ISBN 9798612363897

# Introduction

Mr. Pigglesworth, the money saving pig, wants to help you reflect and achieve success in your mindful money habits. This interactive workbook takes you through a series of exercises to work through money consumption, wishlist, goals, impulse buys, promises, budgeting, without limits and the influence of media. Using this workbook on a daily basis, will help you keep track of the milestones you have completed and what also lies ahead on your mindful money journey.

With this guided interactive workbook, you can reflect, achieve and be in command of your mindful money habits in your life. Each section in this workbook is created to help you be aware of your spending habits while encouraging you to consider the possibilities to improve your saving skills.

# *STOP!*

STOP and think about how to better structure your mindful money habits with this useful acronym. STOP will help you throughout this workbook, when reflecting  and writing in the different sections.

**S**ave for future goals; you'll be more motivated

**T**hrive with saving money; feel good about saving

**O**nly spend what you can afford; find a balance

**P**rotect what money you have; set spending goals

# Money Consumption

Since money is often hard to come by and often harder to keep, mindful money practices should be put into place. While asking yourself, "Will buying this bring me joy because I need it?" It is also important to ask yourself , "Is the act of shopping bringing me joy or is it the item I need?" Sometimes it is the act of shopping that bring us happiness, which causes buyer's remorse after the activity is complete. In order to be more mindful of your spending habits, try understanding the *why* behind the act of shopping for something.

When spending money is necessary, practicing mindfulness skills, like using our five senses when enjoying the lunch you just bought, can aid in deciding where your money should be spent. If consuming the item, such as drink, food, or wearing a top no longer brings you joy, then why are you still buying it? You can put that saved money towards something that can really bring you joy, just not spending out of habit. Remember this is mindful money habits!

So you can better understand where and what you spend your money on, consider writing it down into categories.

## Spending Categories

| Entertainment | Food | Clothes | Other |
| --- | --- | --- | --- |
|  |  |  |  |

# Wishlist

A wishlist is a list of smaller items that are usually $50 and under you want to buy in the future. Keeping a wishlist of top five items you wish to purchase when you have saved money is a great idea as this list will help you buy the things you wanted and avoid impulse purchases.

Most shopping websites offer the wishlist service where you can save items for a later date. The benefit of this is you can often get alerts if there is a price drop on an item. This helps you save even more money and helps you in being mindful what items to spend the money on.

Wishlists are useful incentives for reaching certain saving goals and making saving a positively looked upon habit, rather than a chore. They are also great to have around when someone asks you what you want for a gift. This way you always have an idea in mind and you can often receive what you hoped for without wasting time and money.

1.

2.

3.

4.

5.

# Goals

Mindful money goals are for larger purchases that usually take months to years to save for these items. Having a list of top five mindful money goals can help you save up for those bigger purchases you want in the future. Planning on getting your licence? Maybe you need to save for a car and insurance. What about living on residence for post-secondary education? Decorating your dorm room makes it feel more like home. Perhaps you want to travel? Get a pet? Although these goals seem far away in the future, it is always smart to start thinking about them so you are mindful spending and saving your money throughout the year.

*Stash of Extra Cash*

Better to be prepared than to be caught off guard, when you really need it for emergencies.  Make a habit of putting away some cash for emergencies. You can easily start this mindful money habit by saving the change you received from that wishlist purchase or rounding up a purchase price. This may not seem like much savings, but if you continually practice this habit then the money will keep growing into a nice stash of extra cash!

1.

2.

3.

4.

5.

# Impulse Buys

Impulse buys happen, it is how you recover from the buy that's important. What will you do next time? Is there self-checkout lanes that can help you avoid staring at the "impulse buy" items while waiting in a longer line? Can you carry that item around the store for a bit and then put it back? Often just holding the item for a while will help the item lose it's enchantment.

Our culture is centred around instant gratification, this feeds into the reason for impulse spending. If we can use this idea to our advantage then we can realize we can turn saving into a 'game' of gratification. Just make sure that you make your rules for the game attainable within a reasonable about of time. For example, you aim to save $50 by the end the month. Half you will put into a savings account for a larger purchase and the other half you can use to spend on an experience. An experience is key because it can involve other people, which will help with the gratification role we talked about earlier.  If you don't meet the saving goal then you can do the experience next month when you saved even more. Try not to reward yourself for not making a goal, rather use this time to reflect mindfully on your money habits.

Writing down a list of impulse buys from the past can help you lessen the non-essential and non-goal buys in the future.

1.

2.

3.

4.

5.

<u>Promises</u>

When looking back on your wishlist, goals and impulse buys
sections that you filled out earlier, do you notice any trends?
Think about what you can change or modify to help you reach
these different goals. What strategies and promises will you make
for yourself to practice mindful money habits to achieve these
goals?

Can you list at least five promises you will make for yourself? How
will you achieve these promises? These promises you make to
yourself will help reduce anxiety around money matters and
spending habits.

1.

2.

3.

4.

5.

# Budgeting

Use the following pages to help create a budget. Remember to include your wishlist and your goals while making your budget as this will help keep you on track. Write down your income and expenses to see the difference each month. If you are spending more than you make, then you need to cut back in your expenses! If you are finding you have a positive difference, then you can start saving for those larger goals.

# Monthly Budget

Income:

Known Monthly Expenses

| Description | Date Due | Amount | Paid? |
|---|---|---|---|
| Phone Bill | End of Month | $100 | ✓ |
|  |  |  |  |
|  |  |  |  |
|  |  |  |  |
|  |  |  |  |
|  |  |  |  |
|  |  |  |  |
|  |  |  |  |
|  |  |  |  |

Total Expenses:

Income – Total Expenses =

# Monthly Budget

*Income:*

*Known Monthly Expenses*

| Description | Date Due | Amount | Paid? |
|---|---|---|---|
| Phone Bill | End of Month | $100 | ✓ |
|  |  |  |  |
|  |  |  |  |
|  |  |  |  |
|  |  |  |  |
|  |  |  |  |
|  |  |  |  |
|  |  |  |  |
|  |  |  |  |

*Total Expenses:*

*Income – Total Expenses =*

# Monthly Budget

Income:

## Known Monthly Expenses

| Description | Date Due | Amount | Paid? |
| --- | --- | --- | --- |
| Phone Bill | End of Month | $100 | ✓ |
|  |  |  |  |
|  |  |  |  |
|  |  |  |  |
|  |  |  |  |
|  |  |  |  |
|  |  |  |  |
|  |  |  |  |
|  |  |  |  |

Total Expenses:

Income − Total Expenses =

# Monthly Budget

Income:

Known Monthly Expenses

| Description | Date Due | Amount | Paid? |
| --- | --- | --- | --- |
| Phone Bill | End of Month | $100 | ✓ |
|  |  |  |  |
|  |  |  |  |
|  |  |  |  |
|  |  |  |  |
|  |  |  |  |
|  |  |  |  |
|  |  |  |  |
|  |  |  |  |

Total Expenses:

Income – Total Expenses =

# Monthly Budget

Income:

Known Monthly Expenses

| Description | Date Due | Amount | Paid? |
|---|---|---|---|
| Phone Bill | End of Month | $100 | ✓ |
|  |  |  |  |
|  |  |  |  |
|  |  |  |  |
|  |  |  |  |
|  |  |  |  |
|  |  |  |  |
|  |  |  |  |
|  |  |  |  |

Total Expenses:

Income − Total Expenses =

# Monthly Budget

*Income:*

*Known Monthly Expenses*

| Description | Date Due | Amount | Paid? |
|---|---|---|---|
| Phone Bill | End of Month | $100 | ✓ |
| | | | |
| | | | |
| | | | |
| | | | |
| | | | |
| | | | |
| | | | |
| | | | |

*Total Expenses:*

*Income − Total Expenses =*

# Monthly Budget

Income:

Known Monthly Expenses

| Description | Date Due | Amount | Paid? |
| --- | --- | --- | --- |
| Phone Bill | End of Month | $100 | ✓ |
|  |  |  |  |
|  |  |  |  |
|  |  |  |  |
|  |  |  |  |
|  |  |  |  |
|  |  |  |  |
|  |  |  |  |
|  |  |  |  |

Total Expenses:

Income - Total Expenses =

# Monthly Budget

Income:

Known Monthly Expenses

| Description | Date Due | Amount | Paid? |
|---|---|---|---|
| Phone Bill | End of Month | $100 | ✓ |
|  |  |  |  |
|  |  |  |  |
|  |  |  |  |
|  |  |  |  |
|  |  |  |  |
|  |  |  |  |
|  |  |  |  |
|  |  |  |  |

Total Expenses:

Income − Total Expenses =

# Monthly Budget

Income:

Known Monthly Expenses

| Description | Date Due | Amount | Paid? |
| --- | --- | --- | --- |
| Phone Bill | End of Month | $100 | ✓ |
| | | | |
| | | | |
| | | | |
| | | | |
| | | | |
| | | | |
| | | | |
| | | | |

Total Expenses:

Income - Total Expenses =

# Monthly Budget

Income:


Known Monthly Expenses

| Description | Date Due | Amount | Paid? |
| --- | --- | --- | --- |
| Phone Bill | End of Month | $100 | ✓ |
|  |  |  |  |
|  |  |  |  |
|  |  |  |  |
|  |  |  |  |
|  |  |  |  |
|  |  |  |  |
|  |  |  |  |
|  |  |  |  |


Total Expenses:


Income – Total Expenses =

# Monthly Budget

Income:

Known Monthly Expenses

| Description | Date Due | Amount | Paid? |
| --- | --- | --- | --- |
| Phone Bill | End of Month | $100 | ✓ |
|  |  |  |  |
|  |  |  |  |
|  |  |  |  |
|  |  |  |  |
|  |  |  |  |
|  |  |  |  |
|  |  |  |  |
|  |  |  |  |

Total Expenses:

Income - Total Expenses =

# Monthly Budget

Income:


Known Monthly Expenses

| Description | Date Due | Amount | Paid? |
|---|---|---|---|
| Phone Bill | End of Month | $100 | ✓ |
| | | | |
| | | | |
| | | | |
| | | | |
| | | | |
| | | | |
| | | | |
| | | | |


Total Expenses:


Income – Total Expenses =

Money is only a tool.
It will take you
wherever you wish,
but it will not
replace you
as the driver.
—Ayn Rand

# Without Limits

Often money needs to be spent in order to achieve certain goals you might have, especially ones that you have written down in this workbook. Imagine if money did not matter. What career would you pursue? What would you want to improve? Cure? Create? Visit? Now, slowly get your head out of the clouds because everything takes money but there are ways of achieving those goals without spending *too much* money or very little. For example; say you wanted to help cure a disease. Well, that means expensive schooling and research funding, but volunteering your time to help raise awareness is also a great way of helping achieve these goals. Time is money, so technically you are still spending it!

What are five money-is-no-object goals and how can you achieve them like the above example?

1.

2.

3.

4.

5.

# Influence of Media

This topic can be a book itself. Mindful Money will just focus on the influence of social media and spending habits. Have you ever noticed once you look up an item on a search engine, it suddenly pops up everywhere when you are online, especially on social media applications. The reason for this is your search information is being stored and reflected back to you through targeted ads. These targeted ads are trying to make you purchase the item (like impulse buys but for online shopping) because the advertising companies know you are interested in that item and are more likely to purchase it the more you see it.

Think of five ads you saw recently on your social media. Did you ever search for these items or similar items? Being more aware of what advertisements you are seeing can help you be more aware of what impulse buys you make in the future and how to avoid them.

1.

2.

3.

4.

5.

*N*ow that you have these mindful money habits and tools, it is time to be an agent of change. Push yourself to achieve these habits so that you can harness your power to be a positive impact on the future. Use these mindful money habits to be intentional in your daily life and not just have good intentions. Harness your power to learn, grow and succeed, which helps you create your own integrity. With your new mindful money habits, you can pump up your money muscle and flex your mindful money strength!